MEADOW SLASHER

also by Joshua Marie Wilkinson

Suspension of a Secret in Abandoned Rooms (2005)

Lug Your Careless Body out of the Careful Dusk: a poem in fragments (2006)

The Book of Whispering in the Projection Booth (2009)

Selenography (2010)

Swamp Isthmus (2013)

The Courier's Archive & Hymnal (2014)

Shimoda's Tavern (2018)

Meadow Slasher

Joshua Marie Wilkinson

Black Ocean
Boston · Detroit · Chicago

Black Ocean
P.O. Box 52030
Boston, MA 02205
blackocean.org

Cover Design by Janaka Stucky | janakastucky.com
Book Design by Nikkita Cohoon | nikkita.co

ISBN 978-1-939568-20-5

Library of Congress Cataloging-in-Publication Data

Names: Wilkinson, Joshua Marie, 1977- author.
Title: Meadow slasher / Joshua Marie Wilkinson.
Description: Boston : Black Ocean, [2016]
Identifiers: LCCN 2016042074 | ISBN 9781939568205
Classification: LCC PS3623.I5526 A6 2016 | DDC 811/.6-dc23
LC record available at https://lccn.loc.gov/2016042074

FIRST EDITION

ACKNOWLEDGMENTS

Excerpts from this work have appeared in *Columbia Poetry Review, Destroyer, Laurel Review, Matter, Muthafucka, New American Writing, OmniVerse, Sonora Review, Sugar House Review,* and *Yalobusha Review*. My thanks to rob mclennan, who published a chapbook called *A Little Slash at the Meadow* (above/ground press 2013). My thanks to Lily Brown, Julie Carr, John Cleary, Patrick Culliton, and Forrest Gander for their careful notes and comments on this work. And gratitude and love to Solan Jensen, David Rubin, Abraham Smith, Jaswinder Bolina, Mathias Svalina, ZBS, Farid Matuk, Fred Moten, Brandon Shimoda, Dot Devota, Sidebrow, Black Ocean, Jane Miller, and Lisa Wells.

The italicized lines on pages 8, 26, 35, 44, & 50 are from Andrew Marvell's Mower Poems. The italicized lines on pages 6, 27, & 39 are from Mandelstam (tr. Brown & Merwin), Catullus (tr. Green), and Leadbelly, respectively. The final lines on pages 14 and 41 belong to Flann O'Brien and Shakespeare, respectively.

Meadow Slasher is Book 4 in the *No Volta* pentalogy.

for Lisa Wells

I am a bad place

from whence
to when

a tiny shadow
of that dark
thought

—Eileen Myles

Ein Tagebuch das ich schreiben wollte
bestand aus einem einzingen Satz
>>Ich möchte mich in einen Regenschirm stürzen<<

A diary I wanted to keep
consisted of a single sentence
"I'd like to throw myself into an umbrella"

—Peter Handke (tr. Michael Roloff)

Do your friends know you well enough to pull you through your pasts?

I cut my face in looking.

Dogs on a hunt for what may come.

I am a looked-through garage window where a dead cat furred an oil stain.

A bright April dashing us to the curb.

A gash is how big? A lesion. A slice, say, on the chin.

One of those bruisecuts that boxers get.

I want somebody to come over here & punch me in the neck.

Am I on the phone because I can't end this near a bed or a desk or

anything stable enough to fuck on?

Whiteout. Cold coffee.

Room temperature room.

& my old fall-backs sucked into air

like so many phantoms, drizzled up.

What if what won't

come back to you

is calling?

How much more talk

will it take to sever us?

I'm here on the ground.

Spring drifts away and you chase it

waving your hand like a knife.

Raccoons out, invisible, crunching past.

White heat of late traffic.

I go to the store to buy 150 pillows.

I carry them out to my car, six at a time, three under each arm.

I go from laughing to crying & back

like some stoned, child-weary sitter.

Wearing my quilt as a cape, I'm locked out & it's spring, but freezing.

In my underwear & slippers with just my dog in the street.

I want to get under the empty tables

of the sorority house dining room & huff on some sterno cans

till my head throbs like a stream.

Tickertape firecrackers, a mayor's bald allusion to teenage trysting.

I want now to get stabbed by the wind.

But it's a city with no dependable way out or back in.

So, how bad—you ask yourself—

do you need to leave?

I want what I carried with me

to be enough for over a week.

If in my Sithe I looked right;

roamed rooms, quarter moon.

Wet little pigeonheart

inside me thudding.

Up at Olive & Clark with a tea but

Silver Soul is on & I'm back to it

covering my face with a book, scaring some strangers.

I don't yield out for pity

just a question of what we look like to ourselves

from the bit of future

we're lucky enough to endure.

So it's night.

The shore's lapping.

Heartbreak is having the prepositions

pulse with slashers too.

So then why can't you just gash open a little bit?

A brownout citywide hurricane-grade wind

& I fell in with the chapbook set:

Kassandra's bracketed screams, the ruin

in a so-called net. Well, it unclasps

& I don't want to be here with me either.

What's to learn from what we thought we wanted?

We didn't think we wanted it.

So you've been into the photographs?

What's not desire's aperture.

If the road could stretch out like a blank path under spectral
willows alive.

Or cacti, cactuses—say it wrong with a *w*

I say, low & behold: crawl up into the black dank earth.

What's waiting for us outside?

Some stalled junky in the evening summer

alight under factory lamp blossoms?

It's the West Andersonville neighborhood gardens

& the thieves get a respite. The trains get a respite.

The rain, no breaker. No turn, no volta, no nothing.

Another long thread to pull at in wonder of what it's attached to.

Trying to set down what before I'd carry across into archaism.

An old swamp's widow works the net at the lit lamp of the
    messenger girl.

Are the windows open?

Can't you open them any further?

What scrapes you heals you.

That's not right, but there is a pause before that clippery voicemail beep.

My friends call each at a time

to say, here we are: spent to fire

known to ash, to firetrucks, to the medics looking for something else

to channel up.

What's the right way out of here?

Turn it all up, Dana.

Turn everything up to bleeding.

To summer sun ablaze on the tarry roof with no stars to taser us down.

Is this what we get when we hold the phone to our face?

What did you so want to become

that rent you back to becoming?

I want the curtain to crush the pretty actor.

I want the sets to grow vines into the scaffolding.

So begins the apology's long drawn chain of blowflies out of the bottle

& a metaphor for beasts to know us quickly, what we are—stranded

snared, indefatigable, etcetera.

This isn't for a book of polaroids.

It's to clock the roads of an errancy. An obsession with—

An obsession with what?

With the lamp-lit dust an archive leaves the library shelves with—

But what history did you want back inside of?

Little whale on the Gastineau beach won't last long.

The dream out in the miners' wood, trampling on now.

I like the floorboards in here.

Can I stay awhile?

I'm thinking about retreating to

no trapdoor, no transom, alright. I got it.

Your stripling's looking for a door to a path the way out

like a well-wielded scythe laying down a meadow in swaths.

Pull the quitclaim

out of the old shredder pile for a new terrain.

Check yes or no.

Sometimes I follow the words' sounds' cant, alright?

But I hear it under us—

Stars drifting closer?

Fuck what you wished up.

Your skin won't clean you out.

We aren't who we claimed we tried to be & finally

that white glassy pressure

of looking for something to rattle me

cracks through.

Not like a volt but like

vertical rot

up through the core of an apple—

a ribbed gray worm gorging

is how it felt.

Culpability & subversion.

Some snitch clacking on about community

at the Hideout one night like he's into a carotid.

Sometimes I get down on the carpet

& my dog comes over to see if I'm dead.

I am writing to you

from the watery grave.

You wanna cry?

Cry.

Just don't try to clobber me

with your shitty poems.

Terraplane, milkcow calf,

& some other kitchen blues

through the Cumberland Gap.

I am going to Atlanta, Georgia

to give this gift of bourbon

so I can drink most of it up

& fight my oldest friend to the ground outside Leon's.

A carriage of bladdery heat & we're

running in the rain—

black blood dreaming

in the body.

I'm gonna try

to get off the plane

by climbing out

the lavatory window.

You wanna do this with me?

Get the tape cued so I can

betray somebody in here.

What surfaces

won't let off its oceanic stink.

What you're trading, just functional luggage.

I mean, I wanted to get

lugged out of a well.

Skoal tin of soil, now rain & soil.

You liked to breathe, right?

A good scolding, a hotel room

with one too many freaks to stand it.

Zombies twin in

& the undead rock the rails.

My collected works are

available here & elsewhere

forthcoming. You think

we didn't know

how to find you?

A motorbike headlight's throwing your shadow around.

Funnel clouds, a collective sweat

breaking over the lakeside city.

You hear that crackling?

Beasts.

You wanna learn the way up?

Start elsewhere.

At times a voice in a poem can boxcutter you open.

Blood, intestines, sacks of bile. All that.

Eternal offices of the sore throat.

Indeterminacy is a given

so you needn't start there—

That strangler sure is good at finding abandoned buildings.

Yes & very good.

I make lists & cross off the items as I complete them.

I do this with a line & an x both.

Am I so scared of being alone with the selves I was?

An old acquaintance tries to fuck me on his dining room floor.

Oh, but I want that Bloodbuzz Ohio suit.

Let us un-acquaint ourselves.

I still like it when old folks, rural folks smoke in their homes on tv

clicking between Dog & Hoarders.

What is desire but

some pleasure in careening.

& yet it depends on how you

like it to cadence.

How long do you really like to?

Collated nightly off.

The story begins with you

tapping an unlit cigarette

in the elevator next to your ex—

It begins with Selah's fables

re-told, you know that voice I love the spell of.

What if you don't ever slow down now?

You ruin out all the directions.

That sounds serious.

It's serious, pal.

I said, do you like being here with me presently?

The problem with these half ghosts is that they won't

take the windows out of their casements.

They fail the radios

where they should be interfering like birds

in my apartment.

This intern—trembling—begins to remove

my stitches & cuts me back open, re-making

the wound. What I was

started to shred the fine air

around my body.

How do you feel about memory?

Pretty swell.

You been having a hard time, haven't you?

Enlivened by sadnesses

I'm not playing games already.

This bridge has a compositional flaw.

It goes: half-truth, shitty joke, omit or digress & repeat.

You breathed chalkboard dust intentionally?

You only like nighttime?

You tried & failed, huh?

You know cowardice?

Can I just do what I set myself the task of doing?

Sure you can, coward.

Slowly pulled my hangnail back

just to get a clean rinse out of me.

A *dead and standing pool of Air*:

Each squashed cat or skunk on the interstate I see

I think, what's before us is already done getting itself here, right?

Have your habits grown unkempt?

How shall I answer?

In what register?

You wanna come back inside?

Click through the songs looking for an orchard ladder

to get up into the treetops with.

How did you make your way, young courier?

Tunnel drug lords, a rail track

city garden, a big fuzzy dog

pissing on the flowers.

How much noise did you take in?

I crossed out so much there's

little left to work through—

at the field's edge, after the passing ploughshare's

cut a path through it

A used band-aid's peeking out

from under the wastebasket

in the ladies room & the story

may as well begin here.

A Russian soldier aloft. A flock of weird birds

unwiring us. So, the mail arrives & nothing:

No good postcards for a decade.

Black's fine, but it comes with cream anyways.

& dealing in the trade of alive letters

mis-sent, even the RZA's a cop in some new

primetime slot.

Checked yourself into rehab on Christmas eve.

Your friends—I called & wrote

them—nothing.

City of hash resin, blind kittens, your sponsor.

You know what that sound is?

You know that scurrilous sound?

You know what specious undertaking you're involved with now?

It's the Cumberland rising again.

Let's get Jinx & get down there.

The swallows of the evening

shoot over our raft like melon seeds.

It's alright you didn't write back

unless you still want to. Do you

still want to?

I'm on the computer

just to see if anything

I don't want to go to

invited me out

to turn down.

We're in a Kentucky highway traffic jam

with this old Tammy Wynette station on

& Nebraska's better in Damien's songs anyhow.

Let's stroll down to Hades & turn the box fans on.

You think death jokes are funny?

I sometimes do.

Well, I like your lead apron.

What did you overthrow just to magnify?

How far have you driven today?

752 miles with Johnny Cash,

Roy Orbison & Mr. PC.

Jenks at Danny's. Philip Jenks at the Hideout & Rodan.

Chicago's not wrong tonight, we took

the Damen bus through Bucktown, super snowy.

I want the poem to squeeze

your arm like the blood pressure bag.

I want the dancers to catch

fire a little under the auditorium lights.

Holy turbines, tiny town

known for its college & pulp factory birds.

Spun to scraps, hanged out with the alley slashers

& meadowlark finches at St. Paul & Colfax.

I lit the candle, locked the door & then put my

hand flat on the first step of the stairs down.

Thump of the ghost pulling a face

drifting through bikes

& storage crates out to the night park.

What's your angle?

None to speak of

standing.

Christmas day clasps its fog

condensary to the glossed street hedge.

The sun loses some buildings, cuts the clouds up

like the a.m. alms walkers do to the Tenderloin here

& I'm drifted late in search of

a death to wobble out from.

A child of the hotel registry

watched a man watch a man

at the urinals.

Path grown over & too-low clouds on about us.

The boxer's trainer's brother's in the lobby

with the one he's paid to protect.

Can I have a shot of his hands now?

Your machete's good for a cop ride. Your

pencil's a stump weapon too.

When you slowed to shakes, Alice put you back down

with your red ear to the hi-fi up on Fritz Cove Road.

Terns dropping like rocks, porpoises lifting out

of the bay water, little black bear called your old number

& got your machine.

That not one Blade of Grass you spy'd,

mourning a summer for what it took.

A tree limb hanging almost into your soup, budding

orangey & casting a sunlight spider's

thread to your face. It's morning—

your blouse is open a bit

saying look here, look off

look, look off.

Meadow slashers. Motel drifters

out on the city's lip, lisping.

A ventricle going bully. Heart to

rain & the limit split to georgics.

Hold to the history of

dandelion seed down the storm drain where

you may collect us all as we fold for a dollar, drive

with Abraham toward dusk

& sidle on up for a motel towel.

Thread, gumption, willowy shade.

Some more colleopterous scattering.

Little landlord of the dogs.

A curlew in the postal truck getting a ride.

The child's dreaded publican & fieldmouse arrears.

Mt. Saint Helens, Mt. Saint Arrhythmia.

Tadpoles in bags of water tied to the bikes.

A stubby diving board made from truck tires.

I just want a booth seat & black pints till I climb up to Lethe

or out to Topeka, Dodge City

whence I apparently came.

So, where's Diogenes when you need

a cold friend to laugh you to planks?

The evening padlocks tick open, you

hold the meadow out at a bay of

clannish roads & salt flats scrag

out the planet's dumb whorl to

music in an eye of gin.

How was it falling the way down?

How like a bulb of cold glass

you snapped off into the muck.

You thought your soul careened

crooked?

You thought so?

Rope ladder to a chopper.

A soiled fucker dragging me & mine

through this bad set of dreams. It's how come

your sweated up window won't wake you.

Lingering outside with the song's melody, chilly.

Silver City bound

me and Blind Lemon

gonna ride on down

Bad crosser. A knife in the chest

that ought to hold him for now

while I search up the key.

Spirit thief, your angle is thin

as the lightning insects

its path into your own. Stand down

to suffer fools flung to a current

amidships. The haunted blunder off

through the night watchmen's lit beach shadows.

Notice given. A woodsy clearing

in which to clumsy around.

Yellow eyes turn to position us

in the storm, keeling forth to the breakers.

Here, little storm, is how to get into the grass awhile.

Laphroiag in my red thermos

& my dog asleep beneath the seat in front of me.

The man on the aisle whinging

about his snack bag:

You doing homework, huh?

Not exactly. Exactly what then?

Well...coin-operated moon, watery fields

after tornadoes loosed a split fence,

& some bivouac boards posted up

like placards to the devil mine.

Nor shall Death brag thou wand'rest in his shade—

How slow

can you

fly

this plane

before it

skitches

the woods?

There's a map

on the ceiling

for a way

through here.

Have you tasted the flooring in here?

Can I have a second to respond?

A sort of black pudding, a cudgel,

a re-folded letter. I want the trapdoor

to squeak like a maced troll.

For the windows to just drop their glass.

I keep a good hurley bat near the bed

in case of intruders.

In case of what else?

A cyclone of gnats at the pitcher's face

& it's still Ohio out here.

So who comes in when you sleep?

I want *no scary*—

that's the American version, dubbed.

Press here for bludgeon

press here for steam & here

for marauding-type shit.

Ok, but the rains are coming

so you better get your boots out.

What kind of tripwire have you been

constructing in the off hours? & so for whom?

Your courteous Lights in vain you wast,

The white city drops into a sinkhole.

So let's get sent down there awhile—

chew up our fingernails

& watch the lava pour in

like baked potato butter.

Step down, young courier

into the submarine lazing

in the harbor with

no *Iliad* to attend.

Bring your pencilists, storyboarders

& the child draughtsmen.

Now the wind tips the harbor boats

casting their sails into a cover

over cement quays below a placid breeze

neglecting the tiller now.

I sometimes want the line to

startle a stain off or mark one.

Frigate to trireme, some dinghy or

a lead-ruddered craft carrying

the ferryman's quarterhorse

across a graywhite bog.

What's that the combination for?

Monster maulers to ganglords to subway

cutters stopping for a soft drink.

So animate the border's skeining smogtide out here.

Your socks are too long but I like it.

The wind is called Roy in the short story & he

draggles up his own set of deranged familiars.

How long have you been waiting there

nodding off in the slick

70s seats at the DMV?

When this was in style

it was a hundred thousand years ago.

There was a short orange hammer in your dash

for cracking you out of your car

should a quake find you

in traffic on the Bay Bridge—

Some tools don't come equipped

with a word we'd fear them for.

Not all violence is sad or brutal or funny.

I'm told there are two hundred other kinds

& I'll wait for you in the fog

at Donut World on Judah.

What's beauty but a little death retracted?

Throwing worksite stones

at passing trains

the messenger girl sings the chorus

to the most famous song in human history

by Jay-Z & her rocks

plink off train cars

as they slow through Uptown construction at Lawrence.

As far as I know

there are only two or three ways

for a woman to take off her own dress

without tearing it.

A little music, Monsieur Pain:

If I'm gonna imagine the Green River Killer

Galloping Gertie

the 89 World Series quake

or a samurai sword in the lung

you'd better get the soundtrack together

& if it doesn't start

with Red Apples

& close with Act Nice and Gentle

then I'm out.

For Death thou art a Mower too.

I wrote you an American poem, John Cleary

& it wends through Chicago

to Georgia, from the Mission to the Panhandle.

From Amick's to Buena Vista & back to Zuzu.

You know where I'll sleep tonight—

grow my hair long like that old picture

from *Last Evenings on Earth*.

Next time I see you, fuck tennis. We can just

wander around the ponds in the park for coffee

& a hash brown sandwich. Should we get some sleep?

I didn't think so.

Another good scar

held up to the light

for a photograph.

If the windshield breaks to smithereens

you may as well shut your eyes.

Have you not learned

how to breathe safety glass?

The city may want you to heal

but your friends

all want you

to counteract their fates.

Living with a fuck you at the wrist

but not in the armchair of the scoffer—

I'm with Marianne Moore at Ebbets Field there.

My favorite beer is a sour Bocker

& I drove home a little tipped

from Brouwer's in the rain. Magnusson, Seward,

Gasworks & Carkeek to Golden Gardens—names alive now

from a time when I couldn't be bothered.

Jockeying a life from town to city

& so on to cite them, till me & my dad

were on the third base side for Félix's no-hitter.

Twilight cancels the day—

debts notwithstanding.

What's pleasure but a willed drifting toward excess.

Throw your phone to the side ditch of the river

& the ditch is ringing. No, that's birds

unknown but codified & flown to shrubs, ether.

Your handbag's stuck on the airplane seat's

arm, your frock hem's in the doorjamb, a coin of

chewing gum's sticking you to the floor at

the magazine stand in the lobby.

Waiting for what, little old me?

Alphabet in cursive along a viaduct on Morse.

What's at stake? That would be

desire's rootless claim on the sensory.

My fantasy is so simple it's pitiful:

you turn around & ask me to unhook your bra.

Then, you stand at the foot of the bed

& somehow you undo your skirt.

Your socks don't match. That's

the fantasy? That's the fantasy.

I've been on the graveyard/grocery

bus alone too long, too—

Trying from Kazim's to

get you on the phone since your dad fell ill.

What do you say to the newly bereaved?

Well, what should we say to the dead?

Are you out of hurt & alright where you are?

Can I not know

what up here you're still privy to?

Death's haze on the living

like branch scrapes on branches.

Dusty old sea, I'm just asking

for a ride out to a nearby island.

Come here, school thief:

present the articles of your dealing

today that you may go free.

Nightgowns of snow, but the pageant

continues its lonesome ways into the seats.

The crux of becoming in movement's

memory, memory's blinding chatter.

What were you saying about pity, I forgot?

More ditch ringing

more music against which to crumble like—

Like what, categorizing your wounds?

Like dive off the pier into clouds?

No. Like always swim at night with dogs & a headlamp.

Like design & construct your own coffin.

Like put a pot of tea on & carry it up

the back steps with Pierre Pain & Cleary to the roof in the Haight.

That's your list?

Purity's not a ruse, it's just waxed with tedium.

Meaning the story can begin with a carp flood but

it must end with a memory, some slow

sloping into a whitegreen body of water.

Thought I tasted envelope glue on your bottom lip.

Dialed 1-800-LASER-FACE, to the tune of

I was a master of bloodless experiment

of cottoncandy surrealism & the so-called new brutalism.

Of battletide & conceptual genuflecting.

Master of a blanched line & rye

from the great copper cistern.

Liquor steam? Yes & a cigarette

to fathom the gully breach, nicely.

A quartercask bourbon & the celluloid moon's

show work on Kurosawa's infinite history

of the photographed warrior.

Altgeld to Greenview, Hollywood

to Ravenswood Avenue, where I now reside.

It's not confessional, motherfucker:

it's a constative fact. The rain probably won't

kill you. But could it?

What if joy is embedded not in reflection

but in the bright beams scooping out the highway's

blear? You needn't start there, I know already

but don't we want a little passage?

Out of what exactly? A rustling in

the larches above & a passage the way out.

Funny to think that what I tried to blame my friends for

would corrode me like

old noise trapped in an amp tube.

Well, what armors the birds then?

I know the gar's eye glints white off the face

of the messenger girl's wristwatch.

So you meant, what uses the ocean like a payphone?

Our lord God?

Stood upright with a daffodil—

Leadbelly in the gulf meadow

trailed by children hoo-hooting.